CHRISTMAS

ADULT COLORING BOOK

Bitch

Vol.3

SWEAR WORD AND MANDALAS

COLOR TEST PAGE

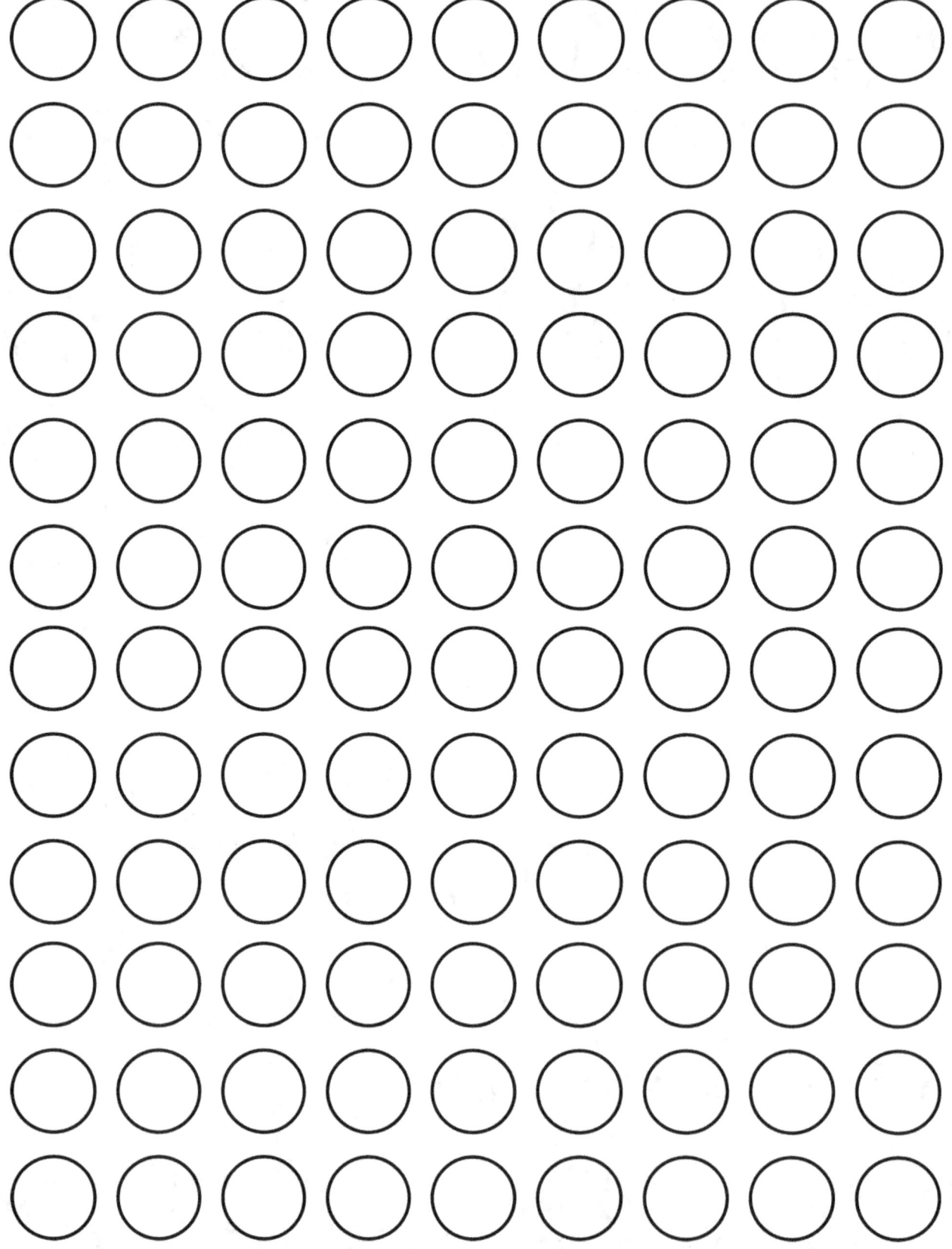

COLOR TEST PAGE

Go to hell,
Bitch!

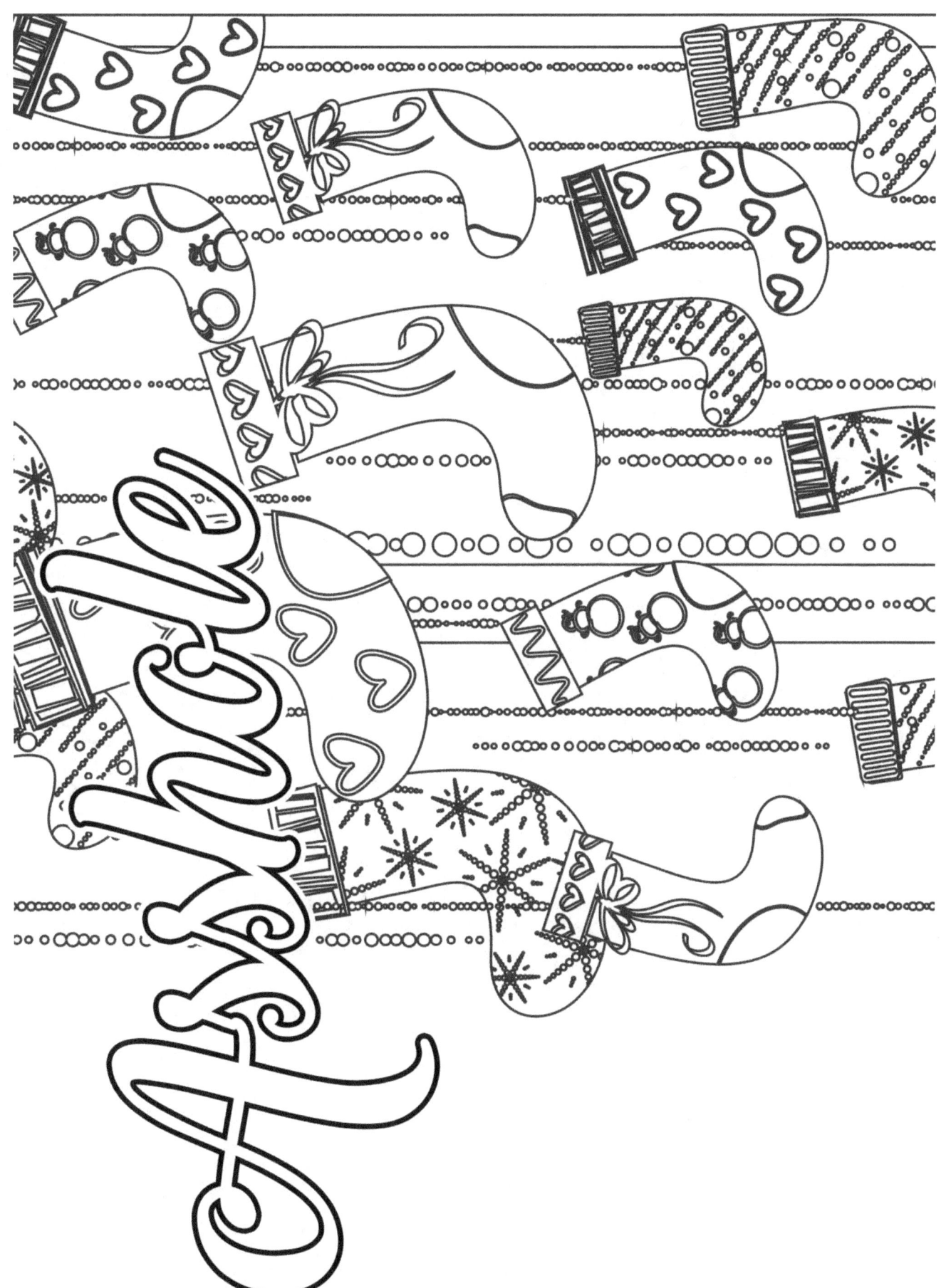

Learn your up it stick up!

BASIC BITCH

www.ingramcontent.com/pod-product-compliance
Lightning Source LLC
Chambersburg PA
CBHW081856280526
45789CB00007B/2719